Woman To Woman

(A Collection of Essays and Poems)

To Caroline,

Relax & Enjoy!.

2/6/98

Woman To Woman

(A Collection of Essays and Poems)

Kim L. Dulaney

Unique Expressions, Inc.
Chicago, Illinois

For information, contact the publisher.
Published by
Unique Expressions, Inc.
P.O. Box 11869
Chicago, Illinois 60611
e-mail: readme4000@aol.com
1-888-README4

Printed By

317-329-9974
Fax 317-216-7148
6212 La Pas Trail
Indianapolis, IN 46268

ISBN 1-891636-01-4

Printed in The United States of America

Illustrations By Ronald E. Deane;

Jacket Cover By "Noyd"

This book is dedicated with love to:

my children, *Kendel* and *Maya*...

and to their children to come...
and their children's children... so on and so on...
with hopes that they might know a piece of me...
a piece of their history.

CONTENTS

Acknowledgments

There is no way I could create a book without thanking the people that have been the wind beneath my wings.

I have to thank :

My parents, *Doris* and *Curtis* - for making the decision to be "PARENTS" in every sense of the word; special thanks to my mother, for coming to me, Woman To Woman exactly when I need it.

My sisters, *Tracey* and *Quintina*, and my brother, *Todd* for helping to create memories that helped to create self-esteem... self-confidence... self-assurance... common sense... on and on...

All of my family, which includes *Dulaney's*, *Thorne's* and *Reese's*.

Each and every one of my friends (I won't dare try to name everyone, because I'll definitely forget someone, and I'll regret it for the rest of my life), you know who you are.

My Bathroom Floor Buddies - *Santha, Mae-Mae, Pat, Janet, Doris, Andrea, Donna* and *Lia.* I have talked their ears off!

Thanks to *Janet* and *Jeri's* daddy (my friends since the first grade), my Pastor at Trinity United

Church of Christ, the esteemed *Rev. Dr. Jeremiah A. Wright ,Jr.* for teaching and guiding me to the path where he knew I would find me.

Thanks to my friend and motivational mentor, *Rob Kelly* for believing and helping me to believe that I can fly!

Thanks to *Tim Hardaway,* my kids' Godfather for remembering where he came from and for trusting Mike who believes in me.

Special thanks to *Mike "Big-Daddy" Reese* for loving me since I was 19 years old, for inspiring and supporting me in all that I desire and for my most precious gifts, my children.

Special thanks to Master, *Kendel Curtis* and Princess, *Maya Micole,* my children for soul stirring inspiration and for making life worth living.

Last, but most important...
I thank GOD for slowing my life down long enough to afford me the opportunity to hear what he was saying to me. He is absolutely, positively incredible!!!! He is "The Almighty"!

Woman To Woman

I Found Me

One day while resting beneath a tree
Without even looking, I found me.
I had been searching relentlessly night and day
Finally sheer exhaustion forced me
    to take a break.
It was just after a storm
    so the ground was still wet
The clouds were starting to clear
    but the sun hadn't shone yet.
I was wearing a white suit
    that had been tailored especially for me
Looking confident and focused
    but was confused as can be.
All alone, drenched with doubt
    and drained by fear
I thought my maker was about
    to take me away from here.
I said "Just in case this is it
    and this will be my last day"
"I'd better chit-chat with God
    to make sure everything is okay."

I started by telling him that I was sick and tired
    of being sick and tired.
I reminded him that I'd been on this
    journey for years, and everytime I'd get a clue,
Up jumped a monkey or two.
To lead me on a wild goose chase
And subsequently cause me to lose my way.
I told him I didn't feel he was fair
I was somewhere out there and he knew where!
Yet, he allowed me to wander around
Searching for something that could not be found!
Finally, when he'd heard enough
Speaking firmly he said "Well, that's just tough!"
When I was passing out blessings
    remember what you chose?
Men... money... cars... and clothes.
You passed up patience, strength and peace
    and wanted nothing to do with knowledge,
    to say the least.
Now you want to blame me
    because your life's a big mess
I told you from the beginning to follow me,
    I know best.
And child don't you ever try to judge me
For without my mercy you wouldn't even be.

At that moment my eyes opened
and I realized I'd been sleeping
Elated I sat there, uncontrollably weeping.
When I was finally able to clear the tears
I found what I'd been searching for
all those years...
Just as beautiful as I'd imagine I'd be
With help from God... I had finally found me.

BLESSINGS
(IN DISGUISE)

Last year while in Hawaii, the rain came.

In my brand new car I caught a flat...
Imagine that.

The storm blew out all the lights last night.
But my garden's growth is out of sight!

My television broke.
So I had to read a book. Hmmm.

The blizzard had us snowed in,
    that's how I got to know my kids again.

Unemployed, broke and homeless
    he found something someone loss,
    he took the wallet full of money
    and returned it to his new boss.

His bachelor party was so live, guess what?
He missed his wedding with his drunk butt.

She searched for more money,
    but he'd exhausted her wealth.
Otherwise, she'd have loved
    the drug addict to death.

Thank GOD!

I See You

I see you over there, sitting in a cut
Hypnotized, while watching my butt

If you thought the swing in my hips
The smile, just beneath my lips
The sparkle in my eye
The sweet scent I left, while walking by
The enticing, caressable curve of my calf
The soothing, mellow, melody of my laugh...

If you thought they were calling you
You're mistaken.
Sorry, Big Fella...
I'm already taken.

One Night's Hidden Treasure

Hair

nails

new outfit for saturday night...   that's right

see my car , as i valet park

cover charge?   that nominal fee?

                  was somebody's lunch money

                      for a whole week

champagne, please.   i don't drink hard liquor

heading home,   money is gone

keep lights, gas, cable,   or phone?

see what i mean?

can't save... don't earn enough money

can i hold $30 till friday?   what's funny?!

Evidence Of Fall

Yellow and brown leaves

half empty trees

jacket or sweater weather

socks

A scraped knee	A bruised heart
tears	tears
fears	fears
comfort from mama	emotional drama
tight hugs	lonely nights
a peck kiss	Vodka with a lemon twist

(+)

One lonely night
Dinner and dancing
She said it only lasted five minutes
A lifetime

Just once... why not?
He was decent enough
Afterall, it had been seven months
A lifetime

Silent phone
He's forever gone
Rumor has it, he knew all along
A lifetime

To freak or not to freak?
Positive - ly
A lifetime decision.

Want A Man? Or A Mouse?

Do you really want a man?
Or do you want a mouse?
Are you ready to allow someone else
    to head your house?
Oh, I'm not talking about a boy
    who's simply up in years
Cause age doesn't make a man,
    let's get that clear.

You like to call the shots, huh?
    It's your way or no way.
Only a whimp excepts that foolishness,
    so you can't mean what you say.

That's right, go ahead and get angry.
    I could care less.
Someone needs to tell your butt the truth
    and put an end to your mess.

Walking around here all high and mighty,
Talking that trash, "I don't need nobody".
You spend all day long disrespecting a brother.
Part of the problem is,
    you think you're his mother.

Quit picking big boys,
    trying to make them men,
Then leaving them,
    and picking the same type again.
And if you think you have a man
    and discover you've been fooled
Leave with a blessing from that lesson,
    and refer him to Sunday School.
Then check yourself to assure
    that you're not running from real men.
Remember they don't all dress in Versace
    and drive Mercedes Benz.

And when you meet a good brother
    don't try to buy him with sex.
I haven't seen a sister
    make a final payment yet.
Like a repo in the night,
    you'll wake up to find him gone.
Having made payments on time,
    you'll wonder what went wrong.

Instead, respect and support him as best you can.
But, most importantly... let a man be a man.

The Bathroom Floor

The bathroom floor is a little saying I created while talking to a girlfriend. You see, whenever I got really pissed about something, I noticed I would almost always eventually end up in the bathroom. I guess it was the only truly private place. People assumed I was taking care of my business in the bathroom. There they wouldn't disturb me or walk in on me. Therefore, I was free in the bathroom. Free to get ugly with emotion. Then, when I felt relieved, I would make myself presentable and re-enter the real world, leaving the ugly emotion behind.

One day, actually while in a happy and playful mood after helping a sister-friend collect herself, I started singing this song to my infant daughter. I've been singing it ever since. I sing it to the beat of an army drill song and I sing it with a makeshift Caribbean accent. You can sing it anyway you like. **Have Fun!**

Late at night when I'm all alone
(Echo)   Late at night when I'm all alone

And everything right has gone wrong
(Echo)   And everything right has gone wrong

I take it to the bathroom floor
(Echo)   I take it to the bathroom floor

And worry with that mess no more
(Echo)   And worry with that mess no more.

How ironic that it would be the bathroom.

Afterall, the bathroom is the place, where you rid

your body of it's waste.

Your Precious Blues

Those blues you're holding on to
Do not belong to you

You think you own them,
    but I swear they're rented
I even possessed them for a brief minute

When I got them, I was surprised to discover
Thirty years ago, the same blues
    belonged to my mother

Since then they've passed through the hands
Of my sisters and all of my honest friends

So I'll say to you what my mother said to me
"Honey, those blues you're hugging...
    they ain't unique!"

They're worthless, mass-produced blues,
    rented day to day
Now... you decide how much
    and how long you're willing to pay!

For those ragged... old... used... blues...

Word To The Wise

Don't
   trouble
      trouble
         till

         trouble
            troubles
               you.

The Art Of Society

There lives a man named History
Who knew a kid named Society

History tells of how Society, as a kid,
painted all of his drawings one solid color.

All black, all white, all red or all yellow
This Society was surely a confused young fellow.
He was the only artist of his day
So no one thought of painting any other way.

Then years later, while in art class
A curious kid named Martin asked...
Why?!
Why does everything have to be one color?
You can't even see the images.

Society, the expert had been painting so long
No one dared tell him his style was wrong.
Society was shaken. How dare he, question me!
Martin continued...

God integrates... when he creates
Just look at this flower
See how God combined red, yellow,
    brown and green
and created the most beautiful flower
    you've ever seen?
Society was furious! He was insulted!
Martin's classmates were astounded.
Martin had been bold enough to say,
What most students thought everyday.

Well, after a long hard fight
    color integration came.
But, poor old Society remains the same.

At least that's the way History tells it.

Food For Thought...

Beauty is only skin deep,
While Ugly is to the bone.

Beauty slowly fades away,
While Ugly holds its own.

WORDS

Can you feel me? I've invaded your body.
I entered through your eyes, but you can't see me.

I slipped into your mouth
and snatched your tongue,
so you won't be able to say a word till I'm done.

I danced around in your head for a while,
but staying in one place for too long
ain't my style.

Oooh, I'm sorry . Are you alright?
You know I'm kinda thick
and your neck's kinda tight.

Can you feeel me, yet?

Now I'm right in your center
spinning my web round your soul,
I hope you don't mind
but I took my sweet time
and patched up some of those holes.
You probably didn't even realize they were there
but there were bumps and bruises everywhere.

Wait, wait, wait. No need to scratch.
That's just me in the small of your back.
Passing these thighs will be a chore, no doubt.
Damn, I see you've been working out!

Now that I've filled you from your head
to your toes,
I guess I'll slip out of here through your nose.

Like a breath of fresh air
I'm outta here.
Like a sigh of relief and you still can't see me
but...
CAN YOU FEEEEL ME, YET?!

PLAIN JANE

The pretentious people,
blinded by bright lights
couldn't even see her.
She stood there... alone
caramel colored
minimal makeup
her warmth would penetrate and permeate
any one who dared see.

He saw her.

Natural hair adorned her head
beautiful body
Real
a dimple here... a slight roll there
nothing surgically stuffed, sucked or tucked
Simple
No glaze or glitter
Raw
Nothing to hide
No need to fake
Boldly, butt naked in her earthy way
Some called her Plain Jane...
He called her often.

Rest In Peace

Life is amazing. A few days ago Princess Diana was killed. Although I didn't know her personally, I felt somewhat bonded with her. As I watched her funeral, I thought about my own life, my children and my purpose. I pondered the question... If I were to die today, would I have done all the things that I was supposed to have done? I thought about how I had wasted time in my life. Wasted time on petty mess. Who went where with whom, and said and did what? I thought about how much of my life's energy had been wasted on a man. Time and energy trying to figure out what type of games were being played this time. Why he did what he did and how could I pay him back?

Well, death will smack you back to the big

picture. We get so caught up when we realize someone or something has tripped us up. We stay in the gutter fighting and tussling. Trying to avenge this thing that has pulled us down. Not realizing that in order to fight that person, we have to stay at gutter level with them. We never really win that way. To be victorious we must get up, dust off and move on. Which is how I try to live my life now in my more mature state.

I've developed a fail-proof reality check. To check yourself just look at your life. Then look at the possibility of your death. Have you made a positive impact on anybody's life? Have you done everything possible to strengthen your children so that they can carry on without you? Have you told somebody, somewhere, in some way, that they are special and that their life was pre-designed for great things? Have you shared your trials and triumphs with those who follow you so that they might have some direction?

Have you done any of these things? Have you let the people who think that you're all that, know how you came to be who you are? Have you told somebody, if only just one somebody, that God can... he has... and he will, make a way out of no way? It's not too late. Today is your day!

When small things get in your way
Focus on these tasks to brighten your day
Then finally, when it's your time to leave
You'll truly know that you can "Rest In Peace".

Tree Of Life

The roots, planted in a foundation

seldom seen,   yet vital

strong, efficient roots bear beautiful fruit

the trunk... big, profound,   definitely necessary

the trunk provides stability

to the naked mind it would appear

that the trunk provides the total lifesource

but,   diseased, infectious roots

will kill the whole tree

A root knows when its been planted

on an unstable foundation

when necessary,

it stretches far beyond it's boundaries

evidence of it's struggles are profound

concrete that can withstand storms

as well as pressure from millions

has succumbed to the strength of mother root

During the fall,   the root rests
the tree loses its leaves
God knows how much one can bear
you have to marvel   at his majesty
he says, "BE STILL AND KNOW THAT I AM"
then he sends rain
come spring...   comes vitality
                              a renewed sense of self

And the cycle continues...

Half Heathen

Today my son behaved as if he'd lost his mind.
As a result,
my thoughts of him were less than kind.

When I scolded him, he started to cry.
I wanted to say, "stop faking you little heathen
and dry your eyes".

I'm sure my face related
what my mind was thinking
as I stared at him without ever blinking

One of these days I'm going to grab this child
and shake him to pieces for being so wild.

Instead I said
"You sit down somewhere and take a break".
"I'll deal with you at a later date".

Oh, no mother, that's not the way!
While writing this poem, I hear what you say.

But the way I handled it was right, I know.
If I'd have dealt with him then,
I'd now be on death row!
(SMILE)

So What?!

She said, "All men are dogs!"

Then she said:

Yes, I drive a Mercedes Benz

Yes, I've got thousands of friends

I'm as good a woman as a woman can be

With a body plucked right out of a dream

I fake as if I have lots of money

Then when I take theirs I laugh, cause it's funny

So what, I pretend to be something I'm not

After "I do", I show them what they've really got

So what, they call me names and kick my butt

I just pack my baggage and move on...
SO WHAT?!

Woman To Woman
(*for* _____)

She was doing it again. Disrespecting somebody,
and herself. I started it as a joke. You know,
woman to woman girl talk. Hee-hee, Haa-haa.

I said, "Repeat after me."

I _____ ,
pledge not to knowingly be with
another woman's man,
just because I can.
I will be selective, discrete and stingy
with my poo-tang
and only when I meet Mr. Right,
will I shake my groove thang
Mr. Right, better known as Mr. Alright,
aka So-So or O.K.

Opportunity knocks...   jokes over
(cont.)

I promise to honor me... respect me...
most importantly, to love me.
I promise to treat me, like royalty
not a piece of property
to be sold,
made old   and cold
Then tossed like trash
all for the sake of cash.

I vow to behave like the Queen that I am.
At this very moment,
I claim the cure over my amnesia.

I now remember...
Who I am
Who's I am
I remember history
I remember family
Great, great, great aunt Sojourner
great, great aunt Harriet
cousin, Mary McLeod Bethune
cousin, Maya
sister, Oprah
grandma, mama and me
Strength...   surmountable strength.

I _____ , clearly understand and accept
the challenges of womanhood
and sisterhood.
I vow
from this day forward
to be the best me that I can be.

We could feel it...
Women worldwide in unity exclaimed,
"WELCOME!"
as their spirits embraced _____.
Woman To Woman. Sister to Sister.

Biblical Quote

As a jewel of gold

    in a swine's snout,

        so is a fair woman

            which is without disretion

Proverbs 11:22

Up FromThe Ghetto

While sitting on the front porch one summer day
The smell of grandma's peach cobbler
   passed my way.
It lingered for a few moments
   just beneath my nose
I sat there, engulfed in its sweetness,
   with my eyes closed.

It was the kind of smell that could only be birthed
from an overused and somewhat abused
ghetto kitchen.

Mmmm, mmmm, good, melted in my mind
While oooh, laa, laa dripped down its sides.
Without taking a bite, I swore I could taste it.
So I breathed deep and long,
   cause I didn't want to waste it.
The scent started to fade
   and just as I opened my eyes
I saw that its pleasure had not only been mine.
I watched it as it floated up and down the street
Delighting and filling everyone it would meet.

This delectable scent went everywhere
It even affected the squirrels that were there.

I watched in amazement as it did its thing
and bore witness to the joy,
simple freedom could bring.

Someday, like that scent,
I'm gonna lie down on air
and spread pure sweetness, as I rise up from here.

Up, up, up... up from the ghetto.

Ancestral Notes
For Generations To Come

Mama said:

If a man tells you -

"I'm no good for you, you deserve better."

- believe him!

Mu-Dear said:

"If it looks like a duck,

walks like a duck,

talks like a duck,

smells like a duck

and ultimately taste like a duck...

then it is a damn duck!"

Zoo Keeper

I think, I thought
he was... going to change
because he loved me
he would
come home at a decent hour
turn his pager off
business meetings that ran deep into the night
would cease
could cease
returning special calls from his cellular
from the garage
conducting business all day
then, conducting *business* all night

Monkey business
working overtime
a snake in the grass
running with dogs
a big kitty
loose
had to be captured
milk the heifer
bring out the gorilla
come home
tame the lioness

I think, I thought
he was... a zookeeper
He was...
Him.

Player - Player

He said, "You won't forget me!"
He was right.
I still remember...
His smile
his style
his smell
his gentle touch
the way he walked
his hypnotic style of talk
his deep voice in the dark
late night walks in the park
the gifts he gave
the passionate love we made.
But, I also remember
that I'm only one of many who won't forget
Which is why
I said good-bye...
                    Player - Player.

Always remember:
> *"Anybody who's loving everybody*
> *Actually loves nobody*
> *Not even himself."*

Fantasy

The sweetest thing...
sweeter than pure honey
raw sugar
molasses
Alaga syrup

Are you with me?

Sweeter than
being awakened by
a warm oil, rub down, at midnight
I tell you this brother's all right!

Stay with me.

Sweeter than morning rain
against our window pane
in Hawaii

Sweeter than a family reunion
in Jamaica
at...   Dunns River Falls

Sweeter than Benin bronze, magically sculpted
Life-like, mahogany wood carvings from Haiti
The motion of a painter's palette knife...
　　　stroke after stroke

Sweeter than a shopping spree, ladies
in Milan
in which... "tu paga"
translation...　"he pays"
Then on to New York
A Broadway musical,　　dining and dancing
A stay at the Waldorf Astoria
with some fortieth floor,　balcony romancing
He's gorgeous,　picture perfect,　absolutely fine
the sweetest thing about this fantasy is...
　　　he's mine all mine.
The sweetest thing.

Big-Daddy

Feminist often get mad at me
because I call my guy my Big-Daddy
I even allow him to carry my bags
and when he pays for dinner, I don't get mad
Here's something else that might sound absurd
He opens doors for me and I don't say a word
Oh, wait a minute, that's not true
I always remember to say "thank you"
He considers me a lady and he's made that clear
Why the other night he even called me, "dear"
He's bought me so many things
    including diamonds and pearls
He's taken me on trips all over the world
My womens' lib friends
    think he's up to something shady
Truth is... I forgot to tell him,
    I'm an independent lady
My friends say "girl you'd better
    let that snake know that you're grown,
and you've been on your own for awfully long"
But I keep forgetting...
    and Big-Daddy keeps doing his thing
I guess that's why he gave me this big ring
Now there you go looking at me all cross
They say with age comes wisdom...
Oh... I mean, memory loss.
          (SMILE)

Have You Ever Seen An Angel?

Have you ever seen an angel?

Well... I have.
As a matter of fact, I have an angel of my own.
He's been permanently assigned to my soul.
His job is to soothe and comfort my spirit.
He does it well.

In his presence I am filled with so much joy
That in his absence my soul still smiles.
Oh, what an angel.

Have you ever seen an angel?

One so pleasing to the eyes
That the simple sight of him
    opens the door to your mind.
Your thoughts whisper... talk to me...
    lead me... take me
Where you are... is where I want to be.

His temptation with your imagination
Brings your body sweet sensations.
Sugar, Sugar, Sugar!
Have you ever seen an angel?

His smile warms you all over
Like a hot cup of tea on a cold winter night.
Mmmm... Now that's tight.

His eyes gaze into your eyes
Through which he sends a tingle,
    to your inner thighs.
Like magic he flows
And you're not even sure that he knows.

I ask again, have you ever seen an angel?

If so, you'd know.
If not, don't stop looking until you find
An angel you can cherish, like I cherish mine.
Thank God for my angel! Sweet, sweet, angel.

Men are indebted to women for two things...

" first for life itself,
second for making life worth living."

MARY MCLEOD BETHUNE

WHO DO I THINK I AM?!

I spoke with a girlfriend who was going through some trying times. I listened and was reminded of a letter I wrote to myself one night. After crying , fussing and tripping, this letter was laid on my heart. I wrote it to my best friend, me. Maybe it will do for you what it did for me and my friends. Best wishes.

3:45 a.m. on a Wednesday morning. I can't sleep. I am awakened by anger and a troubled mind. After having a talk with God I am left with one question...
Who do I think I am?!

The very core of me came from a woman of strong morals and values. A woman who always put family first and who was so giving that it hurt sometimes.
Who do I think I am?!

I know very well that the time in my life when I was flying high and truly at peace was when I was at one with God. I have never experienced a peace like that before. Yet, I get caught up in the possibilities of what society tells me is the ideal life and I put aside all that I know to be true. Then, I have the audacity to wonder why my life looks so pretty on the outside yet, feels so shaky and unstable on the inside. It drives me crazy! I am in a place of uncertainty where I spend most of my time trying to secure things, build equity and invest. As if these things can really sustain me. Oh, of course these things are important. Or should I say they are good things to have? Wise preparation can always help. But, I know that these things alone can do nothing for me. **Who do I think I am?!**

What has made me forget all that I am and all that I know? As I search myself, I come to the conclusion that I am content at work and with my family (mother, father, sisters and brother). That brings me to my immediate family. Whaa-Laa! There it is! My son is healthy, intelligent and basically a good kid. But, I see so many things that he'll miss in my new found lifestyle. He doesn't want for anything material. Oh no. He has it all. But, when I think about the life he's facing I see clearly that the life he's living won't lead him to what I know to be success. All he sees is money as his ultimate goal. He's going to be rich, he says. Play basketball or football, depending on the season.
Well, just **who do I think I am?!**

This is a child...my child! It is my responsibility to nurture and guide him. Not with a subtle stroke, but with a firm grip. Since we're now living with his father, I felt that I could get a break. Let go a bit and leave most of the guiding to him. After all, he has more muscle. He's the man

right?! Well after about a year, I woke up one night, this night, and realized that I have forgotten who I am. Living down the street from the mayor in my man's half-million dollar townhouse of ultimate decor with my original artworks and limited edition furnishings. In the heart of the big city. I realized that I am believing the hype. I thought of the song Gladys Knight sang so sweetly - Midnight Train to Georgia. I thought about leaving on my own midnighttrain... going back to a simpler place and time, to find all that I'd left behind. What had happened to me?
Who do I think I am?!

I was so relieved to finally be with the man I had courted for 14 or 15 years that I lost sight. I was finally getting the prize. Sure there were compromises to be made, but I could deal with them. My son would have his dad! I would have the man that had over the years somehow squeezed through the cracks and found his way into my most private inner being. So, I gave us to him. Really. That's what I did. I gave us to him. I relinquished my total control and gave us to him. Keeping only a small portion for myself. I should have known better. He's only human. Therefore, he is subject to err. Most importantly, he believes he totally controls his fate and destiny. You won't believe this! I gave all that I treasured to a man. A human being. Most importantly, one who does not trust the Lord like I trust the Lord, who has not yet met him and developed a bond with him. Yet, I gave us to him and really expected success?! I expected him to uphold my values and morals? SHAME ON ME! I can't even blame him. SHAME ON ME! When I should have been standing firm and steadfast on what I know. I started out subtly trying to persuade him to come on over to my side of life. When I saw that it wasn't working I got a little closer to the line, and closer and closer until I woke up here where I am now.

Well I feel good this morning. It's now about 5a.m. I've been woke since about 2:15a.m. talking to God, myself and this note pad. This is therapeutic. It really works. God has , in the still of this night, shown me things that I would have missed during my hectic days. I thank God for this day and everyday. I now realize that the only person I should ever give my whole self to is God. I have to pass on to my children the insight and direction God has given me. I still love their father, but I will let him have his fancy fronts and material Gods while I stick to what I know. Hopefully, through prayer and time, he'll step on over and join us, his family. Not on my side, but God's side. It has to be his choice. As for me and mine... there's no other way!
Now that's who I am!!

Hello Sister-friend,

I would like to introduce you to yourself.
Get a legal pad or a spiral notebook. Not the
small spiral but, a regular school size spiral
notebook. Whenever you are feeling strong vibes,
positive or negative, get a pen and the
pad. Write to you. Write exactly what you're
thinking. Don't worry about grammar or
spelling. Just let it flow. Feel free to express your
true feelings.

Afterall, you are talking to you!

You're going to be very surprised at your
thoughts and feelings. Things that your mouth
isn't allowed to speak and your mind
camouflages, will all flow through your
fingertips.

Once these things are on the pad, you can go back
and read them to clear up some of the fog in your
mind.

Eventually, you will see clearly again. Through
this process you will get to know yourself pretty
well. Honesty always creates a strong bond.

**Good luck and best wishes with your new
relationship.**

Kim L. Dulaney